2ND EDITION

STANDARDS CHECK EXPLAINED

KATHLEEN KIRKLAND ADI

WORKBOOK

Contents

DVSA ADI Standards Check explained — 6

What you need to know for the day of your Standards Check — 8

Standards Check Form Explained — 10

Scoring and pass marks — 12

Lesson Planning — 14

Did the trainer identify the pupil's learning goals and needs? – Exercise — 14

Did the trainer identify the pupil's learning goals and needs? – Explanation — 15

Was the agreed lesson structure appropriate for the pupil's experience and ability? - Exercise — 16

Was the agreed lesson structure appropriate for the pupil's experience and ability? - Explanation — 17

Where the practice areas suitable? Exercise — 18

Were the practise area's suitable? – Explanation — 19

Was the lesson plan adapted, when appropriate, to help the pupil work towards their learning goals? – Exercise — 20

Was the lesson plan adapted, when appropriate, to help the pupil work towards their learning goals? – Explanation — 21

Risk Assessment — 23

Did the trainer ensure that the pupil fully understood how the responsibility for risk would be shared? – Exercise　23

Did the trainer ensure that the pupil fully understood how the responsibility for risk would be shared? – Explanation　24

Where the instructions given to the pupil clear and given in good time? – Exercise　25

Where the instructions given to the pupil clear and given in good time? – Explanation　26

Was the trainer aware of the surroundings and the pupil's actions? – Exercise　27

Was the trainer aware of the surroundings and the pupil's actions? – Explanation　28

Was any verbal or physical intervention by the trainer timely and appropriate? – Exercise　29

Was any verbal or physical intervention by the trainer timely and appropriate? – Explanation　30

Was sufficient feedback given to help the pupil understood any potential safety critical incidents? – Exercise　31

Was sufficient feedback given to help the pupil understood any potential safety critical incidents? – Explanation　32

Teaching and Learning Strategies　34

Was the teaching style suited to the pupil's learning style and current ability? – Exercise　34

Was the pupil encouraged to analyse problems and take responsibility for their learning? – Exercise　40

Was the pupil encouraged to analyse problems and take responsibility for their learning? – Explanation   41

Were opportunities and examples used to clarify learning outcomes? – Exercise   44

Were opportunities and examples used to clarify learning outcomes? – Explanation   45

Was the technical information given comprehensive, appropriate and accurate? – Exercise   51

Was the technical information given comprehensive, appropriate and accurate? – Explanation   52

Motoring Firsts   53

Was the pupil given appropriate and timely feedback during the session? – Exercise   59

Was the pupil given appropriate and timely feedback during the session? – Explanation   60

Were the pupil's queries followed up and answered? – Exercise   61

Were the pupil's queries followed up and answered? – Explanation   62

Did the trainer maintain an appropriate non-discriminatory manner throughout the session? – Exercise   63

Did the trainer maintain an appropriate non-discriminatory manner throughout the session? – Explanation   64

At the end of the session – was the pupil encouraged to reflect on their own performance? – Exercise   65

At the end of the session – was the pupil encouraged to reflect on their own performance? – Explanation 66

Review Section 68

Did the trainer score 7 or less on the Risk Management (A 'Yes' response to this question will result in an automatic Fail.) – Explanation 68

At any point in the lesson, did the trainer behave in a way which put you, the pupil or any third party in immediate danger, so that you had to stop the lesson? (A 'Yes' response to this question will result in an automatic Fail.) – Explanation 69

Feedback offered to the trainer (box for comments to be written.) – Explanation 70

Copyright 76

DVSA ADI Standards Check explained

In April 2014, the Check Test changed to the Standards Check. Some ADI's are failing the new Ability to teach. Not just ADI's that were initially Grade 4, even ADI's that were initially Grade 6.

June 2017, the grades of ADI's, having sat the Standards Check are as follows:

- 29% are Grade A
- 69% are Grade B
- 2% have failed.

Between April 2014 and December 2015
- 18579 Standards Check were conducted on 15558 ADI's, meaning that some ADI's were assessed more than once.
- If you fail the Standards Check, you will be removed from the register three times and will have to retake the ADI qualifications to re-join the register.

Source https://www.gov.uk/government/statistical-data-sets/driving-instructor-statistics-ins

Suppose this is your first Standards Check since sitting a Check Test or your first Standards Check since qualifying as an ADI on the PST Part 3 (the ADI Part 3 test is changing on 2nd October 2017) or you are sitting the new Part 3 Standards Check after working as a PDI. In that case, this is the workbook to help you understand the Standards Check.

This book will explain the 17 main competencies of the SC1 Standards Check form, which is how you will be assessed on your ability to remain on the register as an ADI and your grade.

I have called this material a workbook as I have suggested work-through activities to plan your Standards Check effectively.

While working your way through the activities, have a current Pupil in mind; if you are struggling with some of the competencies whilst considering that current Pupil, then start again and consider another Pupil.

The Standards Check needs preparation and careful consideration to gain the highest Grade A or remain on the ADI register in achieving a Grade B. I will explain the scoring for each grade further on in this workbook.

By working your way through this workbook, you can ensure you have planned effectively to obtain the highest-Grade A.

There are many things to consider on the day of your Standards Check:

- Have you arranged a suitable Pupil?
- Have you arranged a second Pupil if the first is not available for any reason?
- Is your car clean? There have been times when Examiners have refused to get into a car due to how dirty the car was. A clean car demonstrates that you take pride in your work. Your car is your office.
- Is your car roadworthy? There have been occasions when an ADI has attended a Standards Check/Check Test, and the car is not in good repair. Either having illegal tyres, lights not working, or faults with the engine.
- Are you smartly dressed? You may think this is unnecessary; however, if you are dressed in sloppy clothes, this can give an impression that your teaching will be sloppy. Remember, first impressions are made within the first few seconds of meeting someone. It would be best if you took pride in your work.

What you need to know for the day of your Standards Check

Arrange to collect the pupil with spare time to arrive promptly at the Test Centre. You do not want to arrive late for your Standards Check.

The Examiner will ask you question's relating to your Pupil:
- The Pupil's ability; beginner, partly trained, trained, full licence holder (new) or full licence holder (experienced).
- The stage they are at in their learning.
- How many lessons have they had?
- Has the pupil had any private practice?
- What topic do you plan to deliver on the lesson?

You need to consider the sensitivity of the Pupil that you are planning to take to the Standards Check with you.

If you take a Pupil that gets very nervous, this may not help you with the smooth running of the lesson. Even though you will tell the Pupil that they are not being observed, they may still feel nervous. Having an examiner in the back of the car can put extra pressure on the Pupil to feel at ease. You may also have the Examiner being examined by his superior sitting in the back of the car, or you may have your ADI trainer in the back of the car, or to make the situation very stressful, all three! Potentially three extra people sitting in the back of your car watching you deliver a lesson to a nervous Pupil can cause the Pupil to fall apart. Then this may also affect your control of the lesson, which can cause you extra pressure to gain back control of the lesson, and you certainly don't want this on your Standards Check.

The next page shows a copy of the SC1 form the examiner will use to mark your Standards Check.

Standards Check form for qualified ADI's

Standards Check Form SC1

Driver & Vehicle Standards Agency

INFORMATION

Trainer Name		Location		Outcome	
PRN		Date	/ /		
		Dual Controls	Yes ☐ No ☐		
Valid Certificate	Yes ☐ No ☐	Reg No.			
		Accompanied?	QA ☐ Trainer ☐ Other ☐		

ASSESSMENT

	Competence
	0 / 1 / 2 / 3
	No evidence / Demonstrated in a few elements / Demonstrated in most elements / Demonstrated in all elements

Pupil: Beginner ☐ Partly Trained ☐ Trained ☐ FLH New ☐ FLH Experienced ☐

Lesson theme: Junctions ☐ Town & city driving ☐ Interacting with other road users ☐
Dual carriageway / faster moving roads ☐ Defensive driving ☐ Effective use of mirrors ☐
Independent driving ☐ Rural roads ☐ Motorways ☐ Eco-safe driving ☐
Recap a manoeuvre ☐ Commentary ☐ Recap emergency stop ☐ Other ☐

LESSON PLANNING
- Did the trainer identify the pupil's learning goals and needs?
- Was the agreed lesson structure appropriate for the pupil's experience and ability?
- Were the practice areas suitable?
- Was the lesson plan adapted, when appropriate, to help the pupil work towards their learning goals?
- Score for lesson planning

RISK MANAGEMENT
- Did the trainer ensure that the pupil fully understood how the responsibility for risk would be shared?
- Were directions and instructions given to the pupil clear and given in good time?
- Was the trainer aware of the surroundings and the pupil's actions?
- Was any verbal or physical intervention by the trainer timely and appropriate?
- Was sufficient feedback given to help the pupil understand any potential safety critical incidents?
- Score for risk management

TEACHING & LEARNING STRATEGIES
- Was the teaching style suited to the pupil's learning style and current ability?
- Was the pupil encouraged to analyse problems and take responsibility for their learning?
- Were opportunities and examples used to clarify learning outcomes?
- Was the technical information given comprehensive, appropriate and accurate?
- Was the pupil given appropriate and timely feedback during the session?
- Were the pupil's queries followed up and answered?
- Did the trainer maintain an appropriate non-discriminatory manner throughout the session?
- At the end of the session - was the pupil encouraged to reflect on their own performance?
- Score for teaching and learning strategies

Overall score

REVIEW

	YES	NO
Did the trainer score 7 or less on Risk Management? (A 'Yes' response to this question will result in an automatic Fail)		
At any point in the lesson, did the trainer behave in a way which put you, the pupil or any third party in immediate danger, so that you had to stop the lesson? (A 'Yes' response to this question will result in an automatic Fail)		
Was advice given to seek further development?		

Feedback offered to trainer

Examiner Name: _____ Signature: _____

C 1/2014

Standards Check Form Explained

The form SC1 is used to evaluate your teaching standard.

The Pupil that you can take along to your Standards Check is either:

- Beginner
- Partly Trained
- Trained
- FLH (Full Licence Holder) New
- FLH (Full Licence Holder) Experienced.

The lesson themes you can cover in your Standards Check are either:

- Junctions
- Town and City Driving
- Interacting with other road users
- Dual carriageway and faster-moving roads
- Defensive driving
- Effective use of mirrors
- Independent driving
- Rural roads
- Motorways
- Eco safe driving
- Recap a manoeuvre
- Commentary
- Recap emergency stop
- Other.

The form is divided into four main sections; Lesson Planning, Risk Management, Teaching & Learning Strategies and Review.

The lesson Planning section is subdivided into:

- Did the trainer identify the pupil's learning goals and needs?
- Was the agreed lesson structure appropriate for the pupil's experience and ability?
- Were the practise area's suitable?
- Was the lesson plan adapted, when appropriate, to help the pupils work towards their learning goals?

The Risk Management section is subdivided into:

- Did the trainer ensure that the pupil fully understood how the responsibility for risk would be shared?
- Where the instructions given to the pupil clear and given in good time?

- Was the trainer aware of the surroundings and the pupil's actions?
- Was any verbal or physical intervention by the trainer timely and appropriate?
- Was sufficient feedback given to help the pupil understand any potential safety critical incidents?

The Teaching and Learning Strategies is subdivided into:

- Was the teaching style suited to the pupil's learning style and current ability?
- Was the pupil encouraged to analyse problems and take responsibility for their learning?
- Were opportunities and examples used to clarify learning outcomes?
- Was the technical information given comprehensive, appropriate and accurate?
- Was the pupil given appropriate and timely feedback during the session?
- Were the pupil's queries followed up and answered?
- Did the trainer maintain an appropriate non-discriminatory manner throughout the session?
- At the end of the session – was the pupil encouraged to reflect on their own performance?

The Review Section is subdivided into:

- Did the trainer score 7 or less on the Risk Management (A 'Yes' response to this question will result in an automatic Fail)
- At any point in the lesson, did the trainer behave in a way which put you, the pupil or any third party in immediate danger, so that you had to stop the lesson? (A 'Yes' response to this question will result in an automatic Fail)
- Feedback offered to the trainer (box for comments to be written)
- Examiner Name and Signature.

Scoring and pass marks

For each of the subsections on the three main sections, you are marked either
0 = No evidence of competence
1 = A few elements of competence demonstrated
2 = Competence demonstrated in most elements
3 = Competence demonstrated in all elements.

The maximum score you can achieve is 51.
If you score 43-51, you will achieve a Grade A
If you score 31-42, you will achieve a Grade B
If you score less than 30 you will Fail the test.

You must score 7 or more in the Risk Management section.
You may feel overwhelmed by the amount of area's you
You may feel overwhelmed by the amount of area's you need to demonstrate effectively on your Standards Check, but don't be as we will be looking at each sub-section individually.

Notes

Lesson Planning

Did the trainer identify the pupil's learning goals and needs? – Exercise

How can you identify the Pupil's learning goals and needs? Write your answers below.

Did the trainer identify the pupil's learning goals and needs? – Explanation

The learning process is a two-way relationship. Instead of just getting the Pupil in your car and say

'Today, we are going to cover Dual Carriageways.'

Ask the Pupil what they want to achieve from the lesson today. They may be struggling with a particular area of their driving that they have not shown to you in a previous lesson.

By asking them what they want to cover, will result in a more productive lesson as they are keen to improve in that area of their driving.

You must agree on a plan for the lesson and work on the area that you and the Pupil have agreed on unless something more serious occurs. (This is explained later.)

- How would you not achieve the Pupil's learning goals and needs?
- Write your answers below.

Was the agreed lesson structure appropriate for the pupil's experience and ability? - Exercise

Think about why a lesson plan would not be appropriate for the
Pupil's experience and ability?
Write your answers below.

Was the agreed lesson structure appropriate for the pupil's experience and ability? - Explanation

If a Pupil asks to cover Dual Carriageways and has not been introduced to Emerging at T Junctions, this is not appropriate to the Pupil's experience and ability. Likewise, if they wish to look at a manoeuvre and have not mastered clutch control or steering in a straight-line forwards, this is not appropriate either.

> Think about other situations that would not be appropriate to the Pupil's experience and ability?
> Write your answers below.

Where the practice areas suitable?
Exercise

Think 'Were the practice area's suitable' and why they wouldn't be.
Write your answers below.

Were the practise area's suitable? – Explanation

You need to use practice areas suitable for the agreed lesson plan. If you are covering Junctions and spend twenty minutes driving on a Dual Carriageway, not turning into or from any junctions, to get to the practice area, this is unacceptable. It would be best to decide on a practice area before leaving the test centre.

Also, if a Pupil is at a trained stage (close to their test), taking them round a nursery route (too easy) is not appropriate either.

If you plan to recap a manoeuvre and ask the Pupil to manoeuvre and the area is not; safe, legal or convenient, then this is not appropriate either.

Remember this is a test to demonstrate your ability to teach, and you want to make the most of the time you have.

Don't drive for too long without covering the subject. Plan the route.

> Think about which areas are not Safe, Legal or convenient to recap a manoeuvre.
> Write your answers below.

Was the lesson plan adapted, when appropriate, to help the pupil work towards their learning goals? - Exercise

Think about 'why the lesson plan would need to be adapted. Write your answers below.

Was the lesson plan adapted, when appropriate, to help the pupil work towards their learning goals? - Explanation

If you agreed to manoeuvre, and along the way, the Pupil struggles with another area of their driving that is potentially dangerous, then this should be addressed first.

For example, you are driving along a road with parked vehicles on either side of the road, and there is an oncoming vehicle that the Pupil did not see and has to stop suddenly and reverse back to avoid the oncoming car. This is a more severe issue that needs to be resolved first. You should then change the lesson plan to Meeting other traffic. Many ADI's feels pressured to change the lesson plan, having already agreed on its goals before leaving the test centre. However, you should ask the Pupil to pull over and stop when convenient and talk about the situation that has just happened and explain that Meeting other traffic will be more appropriate for the remainder of the lesson.

If you plan to take a Full Licence holder and cover Dual Carriageways or Motorways and they achieve their learning goal, you need to change the lesson plan. You need to consider the Full Licence holder that you plan to take to your Standards Check and if you cannot change your lesson plan, you cannot be marked high for this area of the Standards Check.

Think about what other reasons a lesson plan needs to be adapted.
Write your answers below.

Notes

Risk Assessment

Did the trainer ensure that the pupil fully understood how the responsibility for risk would be shared? - Exercise

How will you demonstrate that the Pupil has understood how the responsibility for risk will be shared?
Write your answers below.

Did the trainer ensure that the pupil fully understood how the responsibility for risk would be shared? - Explanation

The responsibility of the driving needs to be shared between the Pupil and Yourself.

The discussion should be something like:

> 'Hi 'XX', how are you feeling today? Are there any reasons why you should not be driving today? Have you taken any medication, alcohol, drugs or are you feeling unwell?
>
> You are in the driving seat and have control of the car. However I am supervising your driving today, and we will share the responsibility. If I need to ask you to take action, I will ask you first, and if this is not an option, I will take control, either by using the dual controls, steering or gears. If this occurs, I will ask you to pull over at a safe, legal and convenient place to discuss where the driving went wrong and how to ensure it doesn't happen in the future.'

You should be having the above conversation with your pupil every lesson, so you can always ask the pupil

> You are in the driving seat today. How will we share the responsibility for the safety of the car for us and others?

You also need to agree with the pupil that you will either; talk-through, prompt or Q&A on the lesson plan.

Once you have agreed on the instructions that you will give, make sure you follow them. If the pupil is struggling with the instructions that you have agreed, i.e. they require more of a prompt or talk through, ask them if they would like to change the amount of instructions you are giving them.

> Think about which situations you would take control of the car. Write your answers below on the next page.

Where the instructions given to the pupil clear and given in good time? - Exercise

How should instructions be given to the Pupil? What does clear and in good time mean to you?
Write your answers below.

Where the instructions given to the pupil clear and given in good time? - Explanation

The clarity and timing of the instructions are vital to give the Pupil the time to carry out MSPSL (mirror, signal, position, speed, and look). A learner takes several seconds to absorb the information you have asked, so you need to give them the instructions to turn further than you would give them to an experienced driver.

The clarity of how the instructions is given is vital.

Alert, Direct and Identify. ADI.

Alert – 'At the roundabout.'
Direct – 'Take the second exit.'
Identify – 'Following signs to the Town Centre.'

If you say to a Pupil, 'Turn left.' They sometimes will literally take the next left turning, and this may be a car park or a driveway.

I hear too often from ADI's I am training

'Go straight over the roundabout.'

This is not the correct use of instructions, and the Pupil could literally go straight over the roundabout. Even if the roundabout is a mini roundabout, this is a contravention of a road sign by not going around the roundabout.

You must agree with the pupil, how much instruction they want from you before starting the lesson.

'Would you like me to talk you through the lesson to start with?'

'Would you like me to prompt you?'

'Would you like me to Q&A you?'

You must then stick to the level of instruction you have agreed on.

If the pupil is improving and you wish to change the level of instruction, you must pull over and then agree to a new level of instruction.

Was the trainer aware of the surroundings and the pupil's actions? - Exercise

What situation would demonstrate that the trainer was unaware of the surroundings and Pupil's actions?
Write your answers below.

Was the trainer aware of the surroundings and the pupil's actions? - Explanation

This is a skill that is an ADI needs to keep the Pupil safe. I describe this as 'Driving on the bonnet.' You need to be one step ahead of the Pupil and other road users. You need to be aware that if you ask the Pupil to turn left, you need to ensure it is safe for them to make the left turn. Also, the Pupil is starting MSPSL to make the left turning, i.e. not checking their left mirrors and checking their right mirrors is an indication that they will turn right and not left as you have asked. Don't let them make the right turn if it is dangerous; correct them before they get themselves into this situation.

Being aware of the Pupil's actions is watching the Pupil after your instruction and coming towards a hazard. If you are praising them for checking their mirrors correctly and they are not checking them correctly, this is not demonstrating the awareness of the Pupil's actions. Likewise, if you are telling them they are not checking their mirrors when they are, it is because you are not watching them, then this is also a failure to be aware of the Pupil's actions.

Was any verbal or physical intervention by the trainer timely and appropriate? - Exercise

In what situations would verbal intervention be timely and appropriate?
In what situations would physical intervention be timely and appropriate?
Write your answers below.

Was any verbal or physical intervention by the trainer timely and appropriate? - Explanation

This is an important aspect of an ADI. It is all too easy to jump on the brakes if the Pupil is not slowing down enough. This is not conducive to the Pupils learning. It can be soul-destroying for the Pupil as they are not learning effectively. You must make verbal requests first before taking control.

Although sometimes when the situation is dangerous, there may be no time to verbalize your request and if you don't take control, this could cause damage or harm to you, the Pupil or other road users or another person's property. This is also a factor to consider in this competency.

> Have you ever had to take physical control of a lesson and thought you could have verbalised the instruction sooner? Have you been too late to take physical intervention and thought you could have done something sooner to prevent this? Write your answers below.

Was sufficient feedback given to help the pupil understood any potential safety critical incidents? - Exercise

What is your understanding of sufficient feedback?
How do you ensure a Pupil understands a safety critical incident?
Write your answers below.

Was sufficient feedback given to help the pupil understood any potential safety critical incidents? - Explanation

Feedback is an important part of the learning process. Good feedback and constructive feedback. It is all too easy to give negative feedback only. This again can destroy a Pupils confidence.

Be sure to give positive feedback where appropriate. Also, be sure not to give positive feedback where it isn't due.

Think about giving feedback as a sandwich:

The bread – give the positives to the drive.
The filling – give what needs to be improved.
The bread – give the positives to the drive.

Thinking about Children, if you tell punish them for being naughty, they may continue to be naughty. If you reward them for being well behaved, they will make an effort to be well behaved more often.

Notes

Teaching and Learning Strategies

Was the teaching style suited to the pupil's learning style and current ability? - Exercise

What different learning styles can a Pupil require to suit their teaching style?
Have you demonstrated different teaching styles to other Pupil's?
Write your answers below.

There are many learning styles, and we each have a preferred way to learn, either by; Visual, Auditory or Kinesthetic methods.

To check your own learning style, take the following quiz to see what learning style you prefer. Sometimes we are a mixture of more than one learning style.

Circle or tick the answer that most represents how you generally behave.

1. When I operate new equipment, I generally:
    a) read the instructions first
    b) listen to an explanation from someone who has used it before
    c) go ahead and have a go; I can figure it out as I use it

2. When I need directions for travelling I usually:
    a) look at a map
    b) ask for spoken directions
    c) follow my nose and maybe use a compass

3. When I cook a new dish, I like to:
    a) follow a written recipe
    b) call a friend for an explanation
    c) follow my instincts, testing as I cook

4. If I am teaching someone something new, I tend to:
    a) write instructions down for them
    b) give them a verbal explanation
    c) demonstrate first and then let them have a go

5. I tend to say:
    a) watch how I do it
    b) listen to me explain
    c) you have a go

6. During my free time I most enjoy:
    a) going to museums and galleries
    b) listening to music and talking to my friends
    c) playing sport or doing DIY

7. When I go shopping for clothes, I tend to:
    a) imagine what they would look like on
    b) discuss them with the shop staff
    c) try them on and test them out

8. When I am choosing a holiday I usually:
    a) read lots of brochures
    b) listen to recommendations from friends
    c) imagine what it would be like to be there

9. If I was buying a new car, I would:
    a) read reviews in newspapers and magazines
    b) discuss what I need with my friends

c) test-drive lots of different types
10. When I am learning a new skill, I am most comfortable:
    a) watching what the teacher is doing
    b) talking through with the teacher exactly what I'm supposed to do
    c) giving it a try myself and work it out as I go

11. If I am choosing food off a menu, I tend to:
    a) imagine what the food will look like
    b) talk through the options in my head or with my partner
    c) imagine what the food will taste like

12. When I listen to a band, I can't help:
    a) watching the band members and other people in the audience
    b) listening to the lyrics and the beats
    c) moving in time with the music

13. When I concentrate, I most often:
    a) focus on the words or the pictures in front of me
    b) discuss the problem and the possible solutions in my head
    c) move around a lot, fiddle with pens and pencils and touch things

14. I choose household furnishings because I like:
    a) their colours and how they look
    b) the descriptions the sales-people give me
    c) their textures and what it feels like to touch them

15. My first memory is of:
    a) looking at something
    b) being spoken to
    c) doing something

16. When I am anxious, I:
    a) visualize the worst-case scenarios
    b) talk over in my head what worries me most
    c) can't sit still, fiddle and move around constantly

17. I feel especially connected to other people because of:
    a) how they look
    b) what they say to me
    c) how they make me feel

18. When I have to revise for an exam, I generally:
    a) write lots of revision notes and diagrams
    b) talk over my notes, alone or with other people
    c) imagine making the movement or creating the formula

19. If I am explaining to someone I tend to:
    a) show them what I mean
    b) explain to them in different ways until they understand
    c) encourage them to try and talk them through my idea as they do it

20. I really love:
    a) watching films, photography, looking at art or people watching
    b) listening to music, the radio or talking to friends
    c) taking part in sporting activities, eating fine foods and wines or dancing

21. Most of my free time is spent:
    a) watching television
    b) talking to friends
    c) doing physical activity or making things

22. When I first contact a new person, I usually:
    a) arrange a face to face meeting
    b) talk to them on the telephone
    c) try to get together whilst doing something else, such as an activity or a meal

23. I first notice how people:
    a) look and dress
    b) sound and speak
    c) stand and move

24. If I am angry, I tend to:
    a) keep replaying in my mind what it is that has upset me
    b) raise my voice and tell people how I feel
    c) stamp about, slam doors and physically demonstrate my anger

25. I find it easiest to remember:
    a) faces
    b) names
    c) things I have done

26. I think that you can tell if someone is lying if:
    a) they avoid looking at you
    b) their voices changes
    c) they give me funny vibes

27. When I meet an old friend:
    a) I say "it's great to see you!"
    b) I say "it's great to hear from you!"
    c) I give them a hug or a handshake

28. I remember things best by:
    a) writing notes or keeping printed details
    b) saying them aloud or repeating words and key points in my head
    c) doing and practicing the activity or imagining it being done

29. If I have to complain about faulty goods, I am most comfortable:
    a) writing a letter
    b) complaining over the phone
    c) taking the item back to the store or posting it to head office

30. I tend to say:
    a) I see what you mean
    b) I hear what you are saying
    c) I know how you feel

The questionnaire will ascertain if you learn by; Visual, Auditory or Kinesthetic style. If you scored mostly A, you are a visual learner, if you mainly scored B, you are an auditory learner and if you mainly scored C, you are a kinesthetic learner.

- Someone with a Visual learning style prefers seeing or observing things, including pictures, diagrams, demonstrations, displays, handouts, films, flip-chart, etc. These people will use phrases such as 'show me, 'let's have a look at that and will be best able to perform a new task after reading the instructions or watching someone else do it first. These are the people who will work from lists and written directions and instructions.

- Someone with an Auditory learning style prefers the transfer of information through listening: to the spoken word, of self or others, of sounds and noises. These people will use phrases such as 'tell me',Let's talk it over and will be best able to perform a new task after listening to instructions from an expert. These are the people who are happy being given spoken instructions over the telephone and can remember all the words to songs that they hear!

- Someone with a Kinesthetic learning style prefers physical experience - touching, feeling, holding, doing, practical hands-on experiences. These people will use phrases such as 'let me try, 'how do you feel?' and will be best able to perform a new task by going ahead and trying it out, learning as they go. These people like to experiment hands-on and never look at the instructions first!

    Record your findings of the self-assessment test below. Do the results surprise you?

When teaching a Pupil, you can use several different methods;

You can offer a demonstration
You can show the Pupil a visual picture and talk through how it needs to be carried out
You can show a video or animated briefing on the topic. If you show them an animated briefing using a mobile device, remember to ask the Pupil to stop on the side of the road and ask them to switch the engine off and remove the keys from the ignition or if your car is 'Keyless', then stop the car using the start/stop button. You are in charge of the vehicle, and you can be prosecuted for doing so. This offence results in six penalty points, and potentially this will result in removal from the ADI register. The Highway Code rule 149 explains this.
Highway Code rule 149
You MUST exercise proper control of your vehicle at all times. You MUST NOT use a hand-held mobile phone, or similar device, when driving or when supervising a learner driver, except to call 999 or 112 in a genuine emergency when it is unsafe or impractical to stop. Never use a hand-held microphone when driving. Using hands-free equipment is also likely to distract your attention from the road. It is far safer not to use any telephone while you are driving or riding - find a safe place to stop first or use the voicemail facility and listen to messages later.

An explanation of this can be found at
https://www.gov.uk/using-mobile-phones-when-driving-the-law

Using mobile phones when driving
It's illegal to use your phone while driving or riding a motorcycle unless you have hands-free access, such as; a Bluetooth headset, voice command, and a dashboard holder. The law still applies to you if you're; stopped at traffic lights, queuing in traffic or supervising a learner driver
Hands-free
If you use your phone hands-free, you must stay in full control of your vehicle at all times. The police can stop you if they think you're not in control because you're distracted and you can be prosecuted. When you can use a hand-held phone. You can use a hand-held phone if either of these apply: you're safely parked (an explanation of safely parked is below) you need to call 999 or 112 in an emergency and it's unsafe or impractical to stop.

Penalties
You can get 6 penalty points and a £200 fine if you use a hand-held phone. You can also be taken to court where you can: be banned from driving or riding get a maximum fine of £1,000 (£2,500 if you're driving a lorry or bus). If you passed your driving test in the last 2 years, you'll lose your licence.

Was the pupil encouraged to analyse problems and take responsibility for their learning? - Exercise

How could a Pupil be encouraged to analyse their own problems and take responsibility for their learning? Write your answers below.

Was the pupil encouraged to analyse problems and take responsibility for their learning? – Explanation

The learning process is a two-way relationship. The learner needs to analyse their problems and take responsibility. Suppose the Pupil is struggling with checking their mirrors. You can ask them to check their mirrors hundreds of times, but if they are not looking at them, they must understand why they need to prevent them. You can have a conversation with them using a mind-mapping exercise.

For example, on the next page is a start of a mind map that you can ask the Pupil more to add to the mind map.

On the following page, create your own mind map.

By asking the Pupil to take responsibility for their learning, they will be more productive. They will also have a greater understanding of why it is essential to check them, rather than just telling the Pupil to check them.

MIRRORS

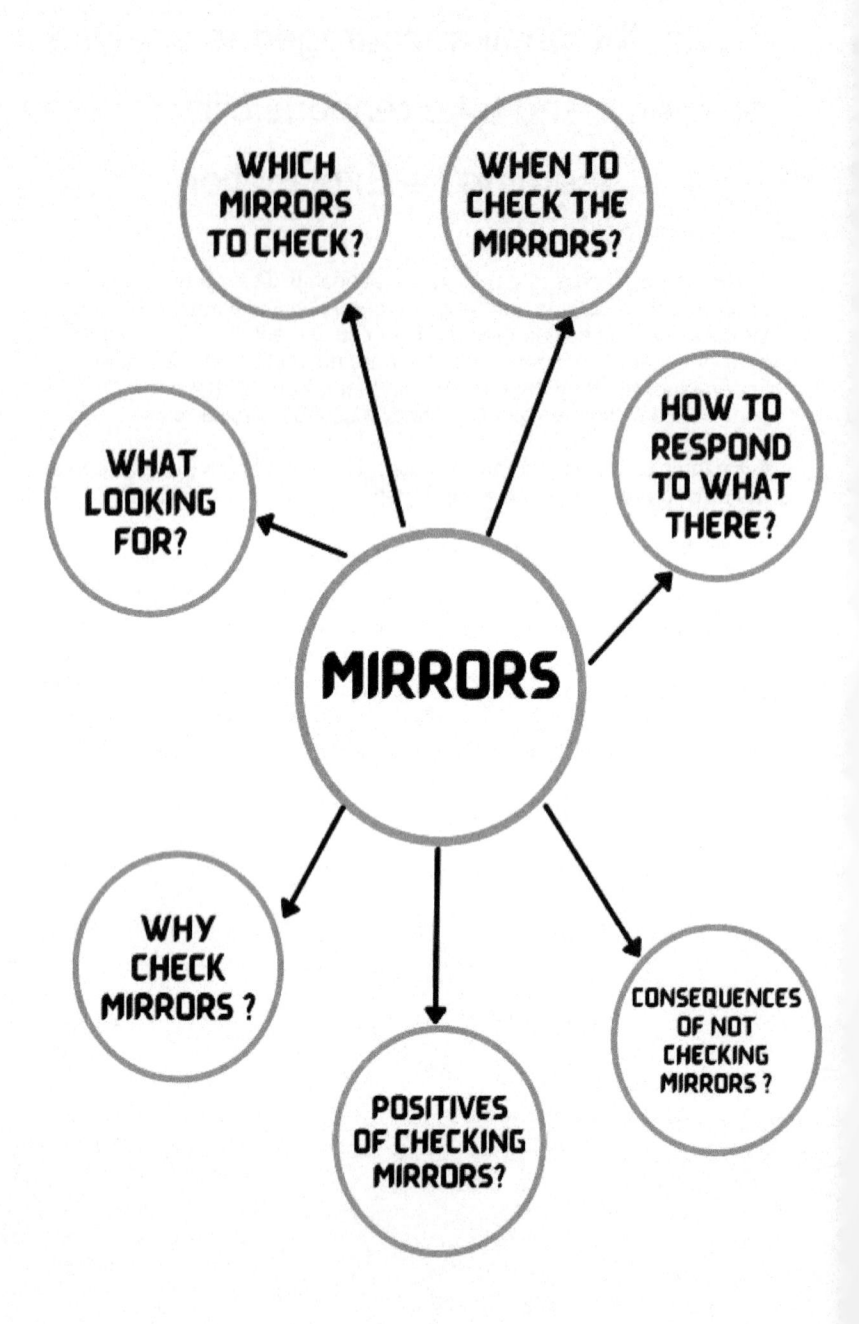

- WHICH MIRRORS TO CHECK?
- WHEN TO CHECK THE MIRRORS?
- HOW TO RESPOND TO WHAT THERE?
- WHAT LOOKING FOR?
- WHY CHECK MIRRORS?
- POSITIVES OF CHECKING MIRRORS?
- CONSEQUENCES OF NOT CHECKING MIRRORS?

Notes

Were opportunities and examples used to clarify learning outcomes? - Exercise

What opportunities and examples could you use to clarify the learning outcomes?
Write your answers below.

Were opportunities and examples used to clarify learning outcomes? - Explanation

It is essential to set learning goals to evaluate the learning outcomes.

The learning goals need to be SMART.

Specific
Measurable
Achievable
Realistic
Timely

Specific
You need to set the lesson plan to a specific task; introducing a manoeuvre or driving on a particular type of road, MSPSL, clutch control etc.

It is not specific enough to say 'We will take a drive' as this is not specific enough. You need to be specific on the areas that need improvements.

Measurable
You need to be able to evaluate the learning has improved. At the end of the lesson, you can use a progress sheet to note improvements to a particular area of their driving. There are also many apps available for use on a tablet or phone. Please remember The Highway Code rule 149 regarding using technology whilst supervising a learner driver.

A sample progress sheet is on the next page.

On the following page, create your own progress log.

PROGRESS RECORD	PUPIL NAME:	
THEORY TEST PASSED		
PRACTICAL TEST DATE		

Subject	Introduced	Talk through	Prompted	Seldom Prompted	Independent
Cockpit Drill					
CONTROLS					
MOVING OFF					
STOPPING					
NORMAL DRIVING POSITION					
CHANGING GEAR					
STEERING					
CO-ORDINATION					
MIRRORS VISION & USE					
USE OF SIGNALS					
MSPSL					
MIRRORS					
SIGNAL					
POSITION					
SPEED					
GEAR					
LOOK					
Junctions					
TURNING LEFT					
TURNING RIGHT					
EMERGING LEFT					
EMERGING RIGHT					
APPROACHING CROSS ROADS					
EMERGING CROSS ROADS					
Roundabouts					
TURNING LEFT					
TURNING RIGHT					
STRAIGHT AHEAD					
DOUBLE ROUNDABOUT					

Emergency/ Controlled stop					
PROMPTNESS					
CONTROL					
ABS					
SPEED					
GEAR					
LOOK					
Defensive Driving					
MEETING TRAFFIC					
CROSSING TRAFFIC					
PEDESTRIAN CROSSINGS					
USE OF SPEED					
TRAFFIC LIGHTS					
DRIVING IN THE DARK					
WEATHER CONDITIONS					
BLIND SPOTS					
Manoeuvres					
REVERSING					
PARKING ON ROAD					
PARKING IN BAY FORWARDS					
PARKING IN BAY BACKWARDS					
PULLING UP ON RIGHT AND REVERSING					
HILL START					
TURN IN THE ROAD					
REVERSING AROUND A CORNER					
Progress					
URBAN ROADS					
RURAL ROADS					
DUAL CARRIAGEWAYS					
OVERTAKING					
Other					
SAFETY QUESTIONS STATIONARY					
STAFETY QUESTIONS MOVING					
SAT NAV					
LOCAL AREA'S					
NOTES					

Notes

Notes

This is a great way to look at a Pupil's progress and improve on a particular area of their driving. Both you and the Pupil should complete this at the end of each lesson. Then, at the start of the lesson, you can recap what areas need improvement from last time.

Achievable
If the goal is set too high, then the learning will not be achievable. Again this can dampen the pupil's spirits of the learning process.

Realistic
The learning goal needs to be realistic. If you have a Pupil who has not mastered clutch control, it is unrealistic to ask them to learn a manoeuvre.

Timely
Is the time frame for the learning to occur in this is unrealistic. If you are asking them to master how to negotiate roundabouts in the first lesson, this is not a good time frame to expect learning to take place.

Was the technical information given comprehensive, appropriate and accurate? - Exercise

What technical information may you need to give to your Pupil? Write your answers below.

Was the technical information given comprehensive, appropriate and accurate? - Explanation

When a Pupil asks you a question, you need to give an accurate and comprehensive answer and only answer if the question is appropriate.

Comprehensive
If the Pupil asks you to explain a road marking or speed limit, don't just tell them

> 'It is because that's the law.'

A Pupil is asking the question because they want to understand the reason.

Appropriate
If you are introducing Moving off and stopping and the Pupil asks you a question relating to a local junction that is not relevant to the lesson today, then you should say.

> 'That is a great question; however, it is irrelevant to today's topic. I will answer that question at a more relevant stage in your driving.'

Accurate
The information you give to a Pupil needs to be accurate. If you genuinely do not know the answer to a question raised, tell the Pupil you are not entirely sure, and you will find out. Also, you could set the Pupil homework to do the same and you can compare notes on the next lesson.

Only answer if you are completely sure of the answer if you do reply. I have met ADI's that have told Pupil's that a 20mph Zone is not mandatory and only advisory. This is not true as the 20mph limit has a red ring around it, making it mandatory.

> Research the history of British Motoring.
> Record your answers on the next page.

Motoring Firsts

Among the questions we are most frequently asked are the various motoring firsts. Listed below are some of the most common questions that have been answered by our Motoring Research Service.

What were the first motor cars?

The motor car was developed over many years by a number of talented individuals but Karl Benz of Mannheim in Germany is normally credited as the Inventor of the Motor Car. In the autumn of 1885, his three-wheeled vehicle became the first successful petrol-engined car. He was awarded a patent for it on 29 January 1886, and became the first motor manufacturer in 1888 with his Modell 3 Benz. In 1886, Gottlieb Daimler and his protégé Wilhelm Maybach built the first successful four-wheeled petrol-driven car at Bad Cannstatt. The Daimler Motoren Gesellschaft was established four years later in 1890. On 1 July 1926 Benz and Daimler merged to become Daimler-Benz AG and its products Mercedes-Benz. Fredrick William Bremer, a plumber and gas fitter, built the first British four-wheeled petrol-engined motor car. Starting work in 1892, when he was 20, the still incomplete car made its first run on a public highway in December 1894.

What was the first motor car to run on the British Highway?

There are a number of claims and counter claims for the first motor car to appear on the road in Britain. Frederick William Bremer of Walthamstow is believed to have had a four-wheeled car running in late 1894. Both he and James D. Roots may have independently built motorised tricycles as early as 1892. Roots certainly had one powered by an oil engine running on the road in early 1896.

Another theory is that the first motor car to run on the British highway was a 2hp Benz Velo imported by Henry Hewetson in November 1894, although some believe this may have actually been in 1895. The Hon. Evelyn Ellis certainly imported a Panhard et Levassor into Britain in June 1895.

By the end of 1895, following further importations, it was estimated that there were 14 or 15 cars on Britain's roads, a figure which had increased dramatically by 1900 to approximately seven or eight hundred! The million mark for private cars was reached in Britain in 1930, with 10 million in 1967.

John Henry Knight of Farnham, Surrey was an engineer and enthusiastic inventor with a keen interest in photography and locomotion. With the help of engineer George Parfitt, in 1895 he created the first purpose-built, petrol-driven, three-wheeled car to be run on the roads of Britain. In order to improve stability a fourth wheel was added the following year. This pioneering British car is on display at the National Motor Museum.

Cycle makers Charles and Walter Santler of Malvern Link, Worcestershire built a steam car in 1889 which was subsequently fitted with a single cylinder gas engine and then rebuilt again with a single cylinder 'petrol' engine in 1894. Santlers went on to build several other cars between 1897 and 1913 when they launched a range of light cars for general sale. Frederick Lanchester started work on a four-wheeled petrol car in 1895 which was successfully tested on the road in early 1896. The Lanchester Engine Co. commenced building production cars in 1899.

When was the word petrol first used?

The term petrol was not used until 1896, when it was patented by Messrs Carless, Capel & Leonard of Hackney Wick.

When were windscreen wipers first used?

There are various claims for the first windscreen wipers. Some sources say that they were first used in France in 1907. British photographer Gladstone Adams is said to have had the idea for wipers whilst driving his Daracq home to Newcastle after watching the 1908 FA Cup Final at Crystal Palace (his team Newcastle United had lost 3 – 1 to Wolverhampton Wanderers). He patented his design in 1911. Various motoring magazine pictures show Prince Henry of Prussia in a car with simple up and down squeegee type wiper fitted to the windscreen in 1909. In 1919 (some sources say 1921) William Folberth of Cleveland, USA, marketed the first automatic windscreen wipers. They were operated by vacuum from the engine's inlet manifold.

Where was the first motor museum?

Britain's first dedicated motor museum was set up by Edmund Dangerfield, Editor of The Motor magazine. Temporarily sited in Oxford Street, London, it opened on 31 May 1912 with over forty vehicles built before 1903 and a range of accessories. The exhibition closed on 31 July 1912 and reopened on 12 March 1914 at the Crystal Palace, Sydenham. The collection remained there until the British Government commandeered the building during World War I, when exhibits were returned to owners, taken in by Government Museums, or dumped on waste ground near Charing Cross Station. This has been described as 'one of the untold tragedies of the war'. In 1931 the remaining unplaced vehicles from the 1912 Motor Museum were destroyed. In 1972 five of the saved cars from the original 1912 Museum were displayed at the newly opened National Motor Museum at Beaulieu.

Who was the first person to be charged for a speeding offence?

Walter Arnold of East Peckham, Kent had the dubious honour of being the first person in Great Britain to be successfully charged with speeding on 28 January 1896. Travelling at approximately 8mph/12.87kph, he had exceeded the 2mph/3.22kph speed limit for towns. Fined one shilling and costs, Arnold had been caught by a policeman who had given chase on a bicycle.

When was the first driving licence issued?
France introduced the first driving licences under the Paris Police Ordinance of 14 August 1893. The Motor Car Act of 14 August 1903, which took effect on 1 January 1904, introduced the driving licence (along with registration numbers for vehicles and a new speed limit of 20mph/32.19kph) into Great Britain.

When were the first driving lessons given?
The Motor Carriage Supply Company of London, their instructor being one Mr Hankinson, offered the first driving lessons in Britain in June 1900. The first organisation to title itself a driving school in Britain was the Liver Motor Car Depot and School of Automobilism of Birkenhead. William Lee established the school in May 1901 and its Chief Instructor was Archibald Ford.

When were the first driving tests introduced?
France, under the Paris Police Ordinance of 14 August 1893, introduced the first driving test. Introduced on a voluntary basis, on 13 March 1935, the driving test did not become official in Great Britain until 1 April 1935 and compulsory until 1 June 1935. The first driving test pass certificate in Great Britain was awarded on the 16 March 1935 to Mr R.E.L. Beene of Kensington.

When was the first Highway Code published?
First published in booklet form in Great Britain in April 1931, it cost one penny.

When did the first motoring fatality occur?

Mrs Bridget Driscoll of Old Town, Croydon became the first motoring fatality on 17 August 1896, when she was run over by a Roger-Benz car at Crystal Palace, London. Employed by the Anglo-French Motor Co, Arthur Edsell was driving at 4mph/6.44kph when he hit Mrs Driscoll, fracturing her skull in the process. The first driver to die from injuries sustained in a motoring accident was Mr Henry Lindfield of Brighton when his electrical carriage overturned on Saturday 12 February 1898. He died of shock the following day, caused by the amputation of one of his legs. According to the 19 February 1898 copy of Autocar, he had only driven the car two or three times and the accident was probably 'due to the fact of the speed being so high' – 16 or 17mph (25–27kph) – 'a pretty high speed for a novice to maintain.' The first crash to cause the death of a car passenger occurred on 25 February 1899 at Grove Hill, Harrow. Major James Stanley Richer, 63, died four days after the accident without regaining consciousness. The driver, Mr E.R. Sewell had been demonstrating the vehicle, a Daimler Wagonette, to Major Richer, Department Head at the Army & Navy Stores, with the view to a possible purchase for the company. Mr Sewell was killed on the spot, becoming the first driver of a petrol-driven car to die in an accident.

When were the first traffic lights installed?

The first traffic signals in Britain (and indeed the world) were installed outside the Houses of Parliament on 10 December 1868. They used contemporary railway signalling technology – semaphore arms for day-time use and green or red gas lamps at night. Unfortunately they exploded on the night of 2 January 1869 injuring the police constable operating them! The first electric stop-go traffic lights were installed in Cleveland, Ohio in August 1914, with the first three-colour traffic lights in Detroit in 1919. 1922 saw the first electrically synchronised traffic signals installed in Houston, Texas. In Great Britain, manually operated three-colour traffic lights were first used in Piccadilly, London in 1926, with automatic traffic lights making their first appearance on an experimental basis in Princes Square, Wolverhampton, during November 1927. The experiment was presumably a success and the lights became permanent in 1930. Pedestrian-operated street crossing lights were first erected on the Brighton Road, Croydon, Surrey in 1932.

Where were the first parking meters installed?

Oklahoma City, USA was the site for the world's first parking meter, where it was installed in July 1935. An invention of Gerald A. Hale and Professor H.G. Thuesen of Oklahoma State University, the first person to be arrested for a parking meter offence was the Reverend C.H. North of the Third Pentecostal Church of Oklahoma City in August 1935. Britain's first parking meters made their appearance outside the American Embassy in London's Grosvenor Square on 10 July 1958.

When did the first roadside petrol pumps appear?

The first roadside petrol pumps became operational in St Louis, USA in 1905. Roadside petrol pumps were first installed in Britain in 1913, though they did not enter into general use until 1921. In 1920 the Automobile Association opened the first roadside petrol station (solely for the purpose of supplying fuel as opposed to being a garage) at Aldermaston, Berkshire. A number of similar stations were established around the country. They were operated by AA Patrolmen and exclusively for the use of AA members. They established the modern pattern of vehicles pulling off the public road and drawing up alongside petrol pumps rather than being filled at the kerbside as at garages. Britain's first self-service petrol pump became operational in November 1961 at Southwark Bridge, London.

When were Cats Eyes (reflective road studs) first invented?
Reflective Cats Eye road studs were patented by Percy Shaw of Halifax in 1934. A manufacturing company, Reflective Road Studs Ltd, was established in 1935.

When were wheel clamps first used?
Wheel clamps were first used on the streets of London in May 1983. At the time they were referred to as the Denver boot, following their widespread use in that US city.

Who was the first person to be charged for drink-driving?
George Smith, a 25 year old taxi driver, was the first person to be charged with drink-driving. He was fined 20 shillings at Marlborough Street Police Court in London on 10 September 1897. Smith had been arrested by Police Constable Russell after crashing his electric cab into the front of 165 New Bond Street.

Why do we drive on the left side of the road in the UK but most other countries drive on the right?
The custom of driving on the left probably dates back to pre-history. It may have been an early road safety measure. At a time when the main danger on the roads was mugging, careful travellers would pass on-coming strangers on the left with their sword arm towards the passer-by.

The keep left rule did not become law in Britain until the increase in horse traffic made some sort of enforcement essential. Before this, the drivers of coaches leaving London for the country simply chose the firmest part of the road.

The main dates for introduction of the legal requirement to keep left are:

1756 – London Bridge
1772 – Towns in Scotland
1835 – All roads in Great Britain and Ireland.

In Europe Pope Boniface VIII instructed pilgrims to keep to the left in the year 1300. Later, class distinction in France meant that aristocrats drove their carriages on the left side of the road forcing everybody else over to the centre or to right hand side. Keeping left had really only ever applied to riding or driving. With the onset of the French Revolution in 1789 and the subsequent declaration of the rights of man in 1791 many aristocrats decided to keep to the 'poor side' of the road so as not to draw attention to themselves. Keeping to the right of the road was also seen as a way of defying the earlier Papal decree.

The subsequent Revolutionary wars and Napoleon's European conquests led to the spread of driving on the right to Switzerland, Germany, Italy, Poland, Spain, Belgium and the Netherlands. Napoleon ordered his armies to use the right of the road in order to avoid congestion during military manoeuvres. The nations that resisted invasion – Britain, the Austro-Hungarian Empire, Russia and Portugal – generally kept to the left.

The Netherlands changed to driving on the right in 1795, but Dutch colonies in the Far East continued the old practices. Denmark had not been invaded by the French but changed in 1793. Russia did not switch until 1916. Czechoslovakia and Hungary were the last countries in mainland Europe to keep left, only changing to the right following invasion by Germany in the late 1930s.

Portugal made the change from left to right in the 1920s; countries with border crossings found there was great confusion if drivers were required to change sides of the road when passing from country to country. Sweden remained on the left until 1967 and changed to the right following a lengthy road safety campaign.

In Austria from 1805 to 1939 half the country drove on the left whilst the other half, the area that had been invaded by Napoleon, drove on the right!

Most of the British Empire adopted the British custom of driving on the left although Egypt, which had been conquered by Napoleon, kept using the right after it became a British dependency.

Pakistan considered changing from left to right in the 1960s. The main argument against was that camel trains often drove through the night while their drivers dozed. The difficulty in teaching old camels new tricks was a decisive factor in Pakistan rejecting the change.

Canada stayed on the left until the 1920s. During the American War of Independence, French liberal reformer General Lafayette gave advice to the revolutionary forces and spread the idea of driving on the right. The keep right rule was applied to the Pennsylvania turnpike in 1792, New York in 1804 and New Jersey in 1813.

Bucking the normal trend, the Pacific island of Samoa made the switch from driving on the right to driving on the left side of the road on 7 September 2009. The official reason given was so as to fall in line with near neighbours Australia and New Zealand which, like Britain, still drive on the left.

Source

http://nationalmotormuseum.org.uk/motoring_firsts

Was the pupil given appropriate and timely feedback during the session? - Exercise

When should feedback be given during the session?
What is an unacceptable time to give feedback?
Record your answer's here.

Was the pupil given appropriate and timely feedback during the session? – Explanation

Feedback needs to be an ongoing process. Do not wait until the hour's lesson is over and tell the Pupil that they emerged onto the wrong side of the road or made the turn perfectly at the first junction they emerged from. The feedback needs to be made at the time of the event.

If it is not safe to talk about the situation at great length at the time, then mention it and say that we need to pull over somewhere safe, legal and convenient to talk about it. If you don't mention the error at the time, once you have found somewhere safe, legal and convenient to pull over and stop and you mention to the Pupil their error, they may not remember. Also, if you mention it to the Pupil, you will not encounter the embarrassment of not remembering why you pulled them over in the first place.

Were the pupil's queries followed up and answered? - Exercise

What questions have a Pupil asked you?
Were all of the questions relevant to the lesson plan?
Record your answer's here.

Were the pupil's queries followed up and answered? - Explanation

If a Pupil asks you a question, do not ignore it. They are asking the question because they are looking for the answer. Remember, if you do not know the answer, tell the Pupil you will look it up and ask them to look up the information also, and you can then compare notes on the next lesson. It is better to research the answer than give out incorrect information. The Pupil will think more of you for being honest if you say you do not know the answer, and so will the Examiner.

If the question does not relate to the topic in hand, tell them we will cover the query in the relevant lesson.

Did the trainer maintain an appropriate non-discriminatory manner throughout the session? - Exercise

What is your understanding of a non-discriminatory manner?
What is your understanding of inappropriate manner?
Record your answer's here.

Did the trainer maintain an appropriate non-discriminatory manner throughout the session? - Explanation

It is all too easy to make comments on other drivers and the quality of their driving, being sexist, racist or referring to types of cars.

If a Pupil comments on another person's driving, disagree with them, instead say something like:

> *'Yes, the driver did make a mistake, but everyone does from time to time, and you do not know that driver, so you cannot make an assumption about them. The Highway Code rule 147 asks to be considerate towards all types of road users'*

Rule 147
Be considerate. Be careful of and considerate towards all types of road users,
especially those requiring extra care (see Rule 204).
You MUST NOT throw anything out of a vehicle; for example, food or food packaging, cigarette ends, cans, paper or carrier bags. This can endanger other road users, particularly motorcyclists and cyclists.
try to be understanding if other road users cause problems; they may be inexperienced or not know the area well.

be patient; remember that anyone can make a mistake.

do not allow yourself to become agitated or involved if someone is behaving badly on the road. This will only make the situation worse. Pull over, calm down and, when you feel relaxed, continue your journey.

slow down and hold back if a road user pulls out into your path at a junction. Allow them to get clear. Do not over-react by driving too close behind to intimidate them.

At the end of the session – was the pupil encouraged to reflect on their own performance? - Exercise

How could you encourage the Pupil to reflect on their performance?
Record your answer's here.

At the end of the session – was the pupil encouraged to reflect on their own performance? - Explanation

At the end of the session, you can ask the Pupil how they feel the lesson went and ask them to scale their performance or progress on a scale of 1-10, with one being the lowest. In your opinion, you can then discuss why the Pupil gave themselves the score they did, either being too low or too high.

You can then ask the Pupil what they need to increase their score.

Use the lesson log and fill it in together, discussing what improvements have been made. This can then be used for the next lesson.

Notes

Review Section

Did the trainer score 7 or less on the Risk Management (A 'Yes' response to this question will result in an automatic Fail.) - Explanation

If you do not score 7 or more in the Risk Management section, you will fail the test.

At any point in the lesson, did the trainer behave in a way which put you, the pupil or any third party in immediate danger, so that you had to stop the lesson? (A 'Yes' response to this question will result in an automatic Fail.) - Explanation

If the ADI allows the learner to commit a dangerous driving fault, a few examples as follows:

- Going through a red light
- Exceeding the speed limit excessively
- Going the wrong way down a one-way street.

Feedback offered to the trainer (box for comments to be written.) - Explanation

At the end of the test, the supervising examiner will make their comments in the box, offer you their findings, and answer any questions you may have.

Hopefully, you have found this workbook helpful, and it has given you an overview of the Standards Check form.

If you wish to have one-to-one Standards Check training before your first Standards Check, you can contact me. My contact details are on the next page.

Notes

Notes

Notes

Notes

About the Author

Kathleen has been an approved driving instructor since 2000. She is also qualified to train instructors ORDIT (official register of driving instructor trainers) and also a DVSA Fleet Registered Trainer. Kathleen runs a franchise to other ADIs and PDIs at her driving school.

Kathleen's passion for road safety and assisting as many people as she can to train to be an ADI as effectively as possible has given her the drive and determination to produce this book.

Initially, Kathleen wrote the lesson plans for her trainees to assist in their training. She then decided to sell it on the open market to help as many others with their training.

Kathleen has appeared in several TV and radio shows in her professional capacity, including 'Britain's Worst Driver', assisting the candidates nominated as 'Britain's worst drivers.'

Kathleen has a massive passion for writing, not only factual material such as this, but also novels, short stories, and radio and TV.

Copyright

Written and copyrighted to:
Kathleen Kirkland
T/A Kathleen School of Motoring
DVSA Fleet Registered Driver Trainer
Kathleen School of Motoring
Website: www.kathleensom.co.uk
Email: kathleensom@live.co.uk
Phone: 0800 24 25 26 9
Facebook: drivinginstructortrainingessex
Twitter: Kathleensom

The ADI and PDI Standards Check Workbook is the copyright of Kathleen Kirkland T/A Kathleen School of Motoring, Bletchley (Kathleen SOM). With payment by you for a copy of the ADI and PDI Standards Check Workbook, Kathleen School of Motoring, Bletchley, grants you the non-exclusive right to use the ADI and PDI Standards Check Workbook solely for your own personal or internal business purposes. You may not copy the ADI and PDI Standards Check Workbook to any third party or transfer or assign any of the copyright in the ADI and PDI Standards Check Workbook or grant any right over the ADI and PDI Standards Check Workbook.

Printed in Great Britain
by Amazon